Navigating *through* Problem Solving *and* Reasoning *in* Prekindergarten–Kindergarten

Carole E. Greenes
Linda Dacey
Mary Cavanagh
Carol R. Findell
Linda Jensen Sheffield
Marian Small

Carole E. Greenes
Prekindergarten–Grade 2 Editor
Peggy A. House
Navigations Series Editor

NATIONAL COUNCIL OF
TEACHERS OF MATHEMATICS

ISBN 0-87353-549-9

The National Council of Teachers of Mathematics is a public voice of mathematics education, providing vision, leadership, and professional development to support teachers in ensuring mathematics learning of the highest quality for all students.

Printed in the United States of America

TABLE OF CONTENTS

CONTENTS OF CD-ROM

Introduction

Table of Standards and Expectations, Process Standards, Pre-K–12

Applet Activities
Making Patterns
Creating Polygons

Blackline Masters

Readings from Publications of the National Council of Teachers of Mathematics

About This Book

Navigating through Problem Solving and Reasoning in Prekindergarten–Kindergarten is the first of seven grade-level books that present investigations designed to develop students' reasoning methods and problem-solving strategies. The introduction to the book provides an overview of reasoning and problem solving as they might appear in prekindergarten through grade 2. The role of the teacher in nurturing the development of students' reasoning and problem-solving talents is presented next. Five investigations follow; each is situated in a different one of the five content strands identified in *Principles and Standards for School Mathematics* (National Council of Teachers of Mathematics [NCTM] 2000): number and operations, algebra, geometry, measurement, and data analysis and probability. For each investigation, the focus is identified, and the activities are summarized. The goals to be achieved, the mathematical connections to the content strands, the prerequisite knowledge, and the materials necessary for conducting the exploration are then specified. All the activities have blackline masters, which are signaled by an icon. These worksheets are identified in the materials list and can be found—along with the solutions for them—in the appendix. They can also be printed from the CD-ROM that accompanies the book. The CD, also signaled by an icon, contains applets for students to manipulate and resources for professional development.

All the investigations have the same format. Each consists of three sections: "Engage," "Explore," and "Extend." The "Engage" section presents tasks that capture students' interest and set the stage for the explorations. "Explore" presents the core investigation. Questions are posed throughout to stimulate students to explore their thinking more deeply about the mathematical ideas. After some questions, possible responses are shown in parentheses. "Extend" suggests modifications of the exploration that make it more challenging or follow-up tasks that promote a deeper analysis of the problem or that require students to create problems rather than just solve them or interpret information.

The discussion section that accompanies each investigation includes comments on reasoning and problem-solving methods and on the mathematical concepts and skills applied in the tasks. This section also offers insights about students' performance and shows alternative ways of representing and communicating the mathematical ideas in the investigation. Margin notes include citations from *Principles and Standards for School Mathematics* (NCTM 2000).

When using any of the investigations, teachers should take note of the appropriateness of students' mathematical vocabulary, the clarity of their explanations, the rationales that they offer for their solution methods or solutions, and the complexity of their creations. Such observations will be helpful in designing adaptations of the investigations for students with special educational needs.

A cautionary note: This book is not intended to be a complete curriculum for developing reasoning methods and problem-solving strategies in prekindergarten and kindergarten. Rather, it should be used in conjunction with other instructional materials.

Key to Icons

Principles and Standards

Blackline Master

CD-ROM

Three different icons appear in the book, as shown in the key. One alerts readers to material quoted from *Principles and Standards for School Mathematics,* another points them to supplementary materials on the CD-ROM that accompanies the book, and a third signals the blackline masters and indicates their locations in the appendix.

Navigations Series

Pre-K–Kindergarten

Problem Solving *and* Reasoning

Introduction

In three landmark publications—*Agenda for Action* (NCTM 1980), *Curriculum and Evaluation Standards for School Mathematics* (NCTM 1989), and *Principles and Standards for School Mathematics* (NCTM 2000)—the National Council of Teachers of Mathematics has consistently identified learning to solve problems as the major goal of school mathematics. Each of these publications highlights the importance of giving students opportunities to apply the mathematical concepts and skills that they are learning—together with various problem-solving strategies and methods of reasoning—to the solution of challenging problems. The hope is that students will gain a greater appreciation for the power of mathematics and for their abilities to wrestle with important mathematical ideas. Neither the mathematical knowledge nor the reasoning strategies can be developed in isolation. They must be learned and used concurrently. Furthermore, problem-solving strategies and reasoning methods are rarely applied in isolation from each other; they, too, are normally applied together in solving mathematical problems.

Problem-Solving Strategies and Reasoning Methods

Students begin to develop a variety of problem-solving strategies and reasoning methods in prekindergarten through grade 2. These strategies and methods are illustrated here with examples from the investigations in this book.

Identification of mathematical relationships

Determining how numbers, shapes, and mathematical concepts are related is central to understanding mathematics. Early in the learning of mathematics, students identify the characteristics of shapes in order to make comparisons. They look for similarities and differences among objects and numbers, and they sort, categorize, rank, or sequence them on the basis of attributes. Later, students differentiate among problems by noting their structural similarities and differences. At the most abstract level, students identify mathematical relationships presented symbolically or in tables, graphs, diagrams, models, or text.

Students gain experience in identifying mathematical relationships in the investigations Bears in the House and in the Park, Shape Families, and Glyph Gallery. Students model story problems in Bears in the House and in the Park and decide whether to add, subtract, or use skip counting or repeated addition to solve the problems. The students base their decisions about which operations to use on their analysis of the problems and on the relationship between the data and the questions. In Shape Families, students identify characteristics of shapes and group shapes by like features. Students identify and compare some physical characteristics of people in Glyphs Gallery, and then they determine the relationships between the characteristics and other attributes, like gender, age, number of hair strands, and preference for pizza.

Inference

Inference is the strategy of deducing unstated information from observed or stated information. Students use inferential reasoning when they formulate conjectures or hypotheses or draw conclusions from their analyses of a problem.

Prekindergarten and kindergarten students are introduced to inferential reasoning in the investigations Fire Trucks and Hats, Shape Families, Line Up, and Glyph Gallery. As parts of a pattern are revealed in Fire Trucks and Hats, students make inferences about the identity of the unseen elements in the pattern. They then determine if their inferences are correct when those elements are revealed. In Shape Families, students analyze shapes and make inferences about how some shapes are alike and others are different. In Line Up, students solve logic problems involving the comparison of measurements. By analyzing glyphs in Glyph Gallery, they make inferences and draw conclusions about relationships between facial features and age, gender, house color, and pizza preference.

Generalization

Generalization is the strategy of identifying a pattern of information or events and then using the pattern to formulate conclusions about other like situations. Students generalize when they—

- identify and continue shape, number, rhythm, color, and pitch patterns;
- describe these patterns with rules in words or symbols;

- predict from a sample; and
- identify trends from sets of data.

In Fire Trucks and Hats, students identify the relationships among the elements in a repeating pattern of pictures, describe and continue the pattern, and then generalize the pattern by representing it with different types of elements.

Representation

Representation is the process of using symbols, words, illustrations, graphs, and charts to characterize mathematical concepts and ideas. It involves creating, interpreting, and linking various forms of information and data displays, including those that are graphic, textual, symbolic, three-dimensional, sketched, or simulated. The process also involves identifying the most appropriate display for a particular situation, purpose, and audience, and it requires the ability to translate among different representations of the same relationship.

Students develop an understanding of representation in the investigations Bears in the House and in the Park, Fire Trucks and Hats, and Glyph Gallery. In Bears in the House and in the Park, students use chips to represent bears in modeling and solving story problems. They also make drawings to show solutions to problems. In Fire Trucks and Hats, students consider various ways in which patterns can be represented, and they identify patterns that are shown pictorially (e.g., hat-hat-truck-hat-hat-truck) and with letters (AABAAB) as the "same." Students interpret diagrams called *glyphs* in Glyph Gallery, and they create legends for existing glyphs.

Guess, check, and revise

This strategy involves using one or more conditions of a problem to identify a candidate for the solution to the problem, checking the candidate against all the problem conditions, and revising the candidate appropriately if it does not meet all the conditions. The revised candidate for the solution is then checked against the problem conditions. The process continues until a solution that matches all the problem conditions is found.

In Line Up, students are presented with three people and a set of clues about the order of the people in a line. The students line up the people according to a possible order that meets one of the problem conditions, and then they compare the lineup with the clues. If the lineup does not correspond with all the clues, the students revise the order and check it again.

Analogy

Analogy is a method of identifying structural similarities and important elements in problems without regard to the particular contexts. Analogy facilitates the solution process because known or easily identified solutions to a simpler problem can be applied to a more complex problem. For instance, if students recognize that two problems are structurally alike and they know how to solve one of the problems, they can apply the same solution method to the other problem. In another example, when students are confronted with a complex mathematical problem, they may construct a simpler problem that preserves the essential features or properties of the more difficult problem. By solving the simpler problem first, the students may discover a solution method that can be applied to the more complex problem.

In Bears in the House and in the Park, students are encouraged to identify problems that have the same mathematical structure and to apply the same solution strategy to those problems. This investigation sets the stage for developing students' analogical reasoning.

Verification

Verification is the process of checking, proving, or confirming a conclusion or point of view. Verification occurs when students—

- identify information that is relevant to, and has value for, the solution of a problem (and when they disregard irrelevant information);
- identify fallacies and unwarranted assumptions;
- recognize that solutions are reasonably close to estimates and make sense within the contexts of problems;
- justify the use of particular solution strategies by convincing arguments or—at a later age—proofs;
- formulate counterexamples.

Students also verify their own solutions when they identify gaps, inconsistencies, or contradictions in another person's line of reasoning.

Verification is developed in all the investigations in this book. In Bears in the House and in the Park, students create story problems, solve one another's problems, and verify their partner's solution. When they predict the identity of covered elements in patterns in Fire Trucks and Hats, students must justify their solutions. In Shape Families, students justify the grouping of similar shapes and the elimination of the shape that is different. Students verify the order of people in Line Up by checking the order against the problem conditions. In Glyph Gallery, after determining the relationship between glyphs and attributes of objects and creating a glyph legend, students check to be sure that all the glyphs are interpreted correctly.

Developing Mathematical Dispositions

It is hoped that these investigations, which emphasize problem solving and reasoning, and other challenging mathematical activities will develop students' love of mathematics and their dispositions to—

- enjoy solving difficult problems;
- make sense of seemingly nonsensical situations or fix or "salvage" vague problems by rephrasing them and eliminating ambiguities;
- persist until they find a solution to a problem or until they determine that no solution exists;

- reflect on their solutions and solution methods and make adjustments accordingly;
- recognize that to solve some problems, they must learn more mathematics;
- generate new mathematical questions for a given problem;
- listen to others and analyze and verify their peers' lines of reasoning.

The Role of the Teacher

To strengthen students' mathematical reasoning and problem-solving abilities, teachers must create classroom environments that are mathematically "safe"—that is, ones in which every child feels free to make conjectures, to explore different ways of thinking, and to share his or her ideas with classmates. Teachers must be able to assess students' thinking and adjust mathematical tasks on the basis of assessment data. Most important, teachers must facilitate classroom discourse and ask probing questions in order to deepen students' understanding of the mathematics and of the reasoning methods and problem-solving strategies that the students employ.

Facilitate classroom discourse

Classroom discourse gives students opportunities to communicate their mathematical reasoning. In such discourse, students explore conjectures and clarify their understanding of problem-solving strategies. Informal discussions among pairs or small groups of students can enhance students' commitments to a task and assist less able learners in understanding the nature of a task, the meaning of the terminology, and the appropriate vocabulary to use in a response. Whole-class discussions serve as forums for students to share their findings, make generalizations, and explore alternative approaches. Classroom discourse also gives teachers important insights into their students' thinking.

Students in prekindergarten to grade 2 often share their mathematical thinking in pairs or small groups quite naturally, with little or no intervention by the teacher. Most young children are comfortable talking aloud as they solve problems. It can be challenging, however, to sustain a whole-class discussion among young students. Nonetheless, teachers can foster such discussions in a variety of ways:

- *Extend wait time.* Students need time to ponder important ideas and to formulate their responses. Don't be concerned if your students don't comment immediately. When teachers wait a bit longer than they are accustomed to doing, students often do respond.
- *Allow students to correct one another.* It can be difficult not to respond to every incorrect comment. Constant correction by the teacher, however, leads students to rely on the teacher as the authority rather than on their own mathematical knowledge, reasoning, and verification methods.
- *Ask more questions.* Instead of always responding to a student's contribution with a direct comment, encourage student-to-student interaction by asking such questions as these: "Did anyone else find

this solution?" "Can anyone help with this question?" "What do you think we should do about this?"

- *Support reticent speakers.* Afford students who rarely comment or ask questions opportunities to practice what they intend to share with their group or class so that they may become more confident. Inquire if they would like to speak first so that they don't need to wait anxiously for their turns. You can also bring these students into discussions by asking, "Would anyone else like to add something or give another opinion?"

- *Encourage the use of recording sheets.* For very young children, recording may take the form of making simple drawings to record solutions, strategies, or merely something about the problem. As students' abilities to record their thinking develop, drawings become more sophisticated, and recordings may include written explanations and symbolic representations. More-mature students may depict more than one solution strategy. The recording sheets give all students something to share and can help young children recall their investigative work.

- *Summarize ideas.* Recording students' ideas on the chalkboard or on large easel paper helps focus discussions and lets the students know that their ideas are important.

Students' discourse is an invaluable resource. It can lead to a deeper understanding of the mathematics embedded in problems and may launch new investigations. It offers opportunities for students to develop their reasoning abilities as they challenge and defend ideas. Finally, it gives teachers insights into students' thinking that can in turn be valuable in making instructional decisions.

Ask probing questions

The questions that a teacher asks during an investigation can help students understand their own thinking. In responding to these questions, the students make links among problems, strategies, and representations, and they check their logic and make generalizations.

Good problem solvers know what they are doing and why they are doing it. They know when they need help or should change strategies. Teachers' questions help young students develop good metacognitive habits. The following are examples of questions that prompt students' reflection:

- "What did you do first? Why?"
- "Why did you change your mind?"
- "What were you thinking when you recorded this?"
- "Which clue did you think was the most (least) helpful? Why?"
- "What made this investigation easy (or difficult) for you?"
- "What do you plan to do next?"
- "What hint would you give to a friend who was stuck?"

Discovering connections among problems, strategies, and representations deepens mathematical thinking and strengthens problem-

"Good problem solvers monitor their thinking regularly and automatically."
(Van de Walle 2004, p. 54)

solving abilities. To help students make such connections, ask questions such as these:

- "Does this problem remind you of another problem that you have already solved?"
- "Is there another way to solve this problem?"
- "Can you create a problem that could also be solved this way?"
- "Can you represent this information in a different way?"

Rich mathematical investigations give students opportunities to develop their reasoning skills further. Students can make predictions, generalize ideas, and recognize logical inconsistencies. Questions such as the following can help students enhance their reasoning abilities:

- "What do you think will happen next? Why?"
- "Do you think this pattern will continue? Why?"
- "Would this still be true if you began with an odd number [*or other counterexample*]?"
- "Can you state a general rule you have discovered?"
- "What will never happen when you do this?"

Finally, through your example, you can strengthen your students' problem-solving and reasoning abilities. Throughout the school day, teachers as well as students have numerous opportunities to exhibit curiosity about how things work and what generalizations can be made, to exemplify good reasoning and the use of varying problem-solving strategies, and to evoke in students the belief that mathematical thinking is an elegant and exciting problem-solving tool.

Navigations Series

Pre-K–Kindergarten

Problem Solving *and* Reasoning

Investigations

Bears in the House and in the Park

Focus

Reasoning about number relationships

Summary

Students model, solve, and create story problems.

Goals

- Model mathematical situations
- Identify problems that can be solved in the same way
- Use drawings and symbols to represent mathematical ideas
- Formulate problems

Mathematical Connections

Number and Operations

- Counting objects in a group
- Modeling situations that involve addition, subtraction, and multiplication

Algebra

- Modeling quantitative relationships with objects, pictures, and symbols

Prior Knowledge

- Counting up to twelve objects
- Using spatial terms to describe the locations *up*, *down*, *above*, and *below*

pp. 30, 31

Materials

- Twelve teddy-bear counters or chips for each student
- Paper, crayons, and pencils for each student
- A copy of the blackline master "The Teddy-Bear House" for each student
- A copy of the blackline master "The Teddy-Bear Park" for each student

Investigation

Engage

Gather the students in a circle and give each one a copy of the blackline master "The Teddy-Bear House." Ask the students to describe what they see. Depending on their responses, you may want to ask questions such as these to elicit a description:

- "How many rooms do you see in this house?" (four)

- "How many stairs do you see?" (six)
- "What rooms do you see upstairs?" (a bedroom and a study)
- "What rooms do you see downstairs?" (a kitchen and a living room)
- "Which room is below the bedroom?" (the kitchen)
- "Which room is above the living room?" (the study)

Explore

Give each student twelve teddy-bear counters or chips. Explain to the students that you will be sharing with them some story problems about the bears and their house. The students' job is to use the "bears" (counters or chips) to model the story problems. After each one, be sure that the students remove all the bears from their houses before you begin the next story problem. Use the following samples, or make up others that are appropriate for your class:

Story Problem 1
There are two bears in the kitchen.
There are three bears in the living room.
How many bears are downstairs? (five)

Story Problem 2
There are two bears on each stair.
How many bears are on the stairs in all? (twelve)

Story Problem 3
There are eight bears in the study.
Two bears leave to go to the bedroom to sleep.
How many bears are in the study now? (six)

Story Problem 4
Nine bears are eating lunch in the kitchen.
Two bears finish and go upstairs.
How many bears are left in the kitchen? (seven)

Story Problem 5
Three bears are sitting in the living room.
Four more bears come to join them.
How many bears are in the living room now? (seven)

Story Problem 6
There are three bears in each room.
How many bears are there in the house? (twelve)

As the students solve a problem, you may want to have them whisper their answers to you or to check with a partner before discussing the answers as a group. Those who are able can record their answers numerically.

Give the students one more problem to solve. Tell the following story problem twice and then have a volunteer retell it:

There are four bears downstairs.
There are six bears upstairs.
How many bears are there in the house? (ten)

"Posing problems, that is, generating new questions in a problem context, is a mathematical disposition that teachers should nurture and develop."
(NCTM 2000, p.117)

Have the children make drawings to show their solutions. When all the students have solved the problem and represented their work, invite them to share the representations.

The next day, give each student a copy of the blackline master "The Teddy-Bear Park" and twelve teddy-bear counters or chips. Ask the students to describe what they see in the picture and then create story problems (using the numbers zero through six) about bears playing in the park. You may wish to record the problems as the students dictate them. The students can write the appropriate number sentences, and you can then record the answers in complete sentences, as shown in figure 1. Allow time for the students to present their problems and solve their classmates' problems.

10 children are in the sandbox.
That's too many.
So 5 go away.
How many are in the sandbox now?

$$10 - 5 = 5$$

5 children are still in the sandbox.

There's a bear on this swing, this swing, this swing, and this swing.
How many bears are swinging?

$$1 + 1 + 1 + 1 = 4$$

4 bears are swinging.

3 children are in the sandbox.
2 children are on the swings.
2 children are on the slide.
How many children played?

$$3 + 2 + 2 \text{ is } 5 + 2 = 7$$

7 children played.

Fig. **1.**
Examples of student-created story problems

Following the presentation of each problem, ask, "Did anyone make up another story problem like this one?" The students may focus on various aspects of a problem, such as the places in the park or the numbers of bears. To help the children focus on the mathematical structure of the problem, ask, "What did you do to solve this problem?" and "Can you create a problem that can be solved in the same way?"

Extend

The students who are interested in a greater challenge could model and solve story problems of the form $a + \square = c$. The following story problems are examples:

Extension Story Problem 1

There are four bears in the study.
Some more bears join them.
Now there are seven bears in the study.
How many bears joined the first four bears? (three)

Extension Story Problem 2

Five bears are in the kitchen.
More bears are in the living room.
There are eleven bears downstairs.
How many bears are in the living room? (six)

Discussion

It is important for young students to have many opportunities to model story problems. This type of investigation sets the stage for introducing the arithmetic operations and helps students gain confidence in their abilities to make sense of the mathematical relationships presented in prose. The students can then learn to link story problems to symbolic representations (e.g., number sentences).

Throughout the activity, observe the students carefully as they model the story problems concretely. The information gained from noting the following behaviors will enable you to prepare future instruction that is responsive to students' needs:

- When combining two groups of bears, do the students count by ones, or do they count on from the number of bears in one of the groups?
- When counting the bears on the stairs, do the students count by ones or by twos?
- When collecting a group of three bears, do the students count each bear, or do they seem to recognize a group of three?
- Do the students count a second time to check their answers?

The process of identifying problems that have the same mathematical structure and applying the same solution method to these problems is one of the most powerful problem-solving strategies; it is often referred to as *analogical reasoning*.

For other examples of activities that develop students' algebraic reasoning, see Navigating through Algebra in Prekindergarten–Grade 2 *(Greenes et al. 2001).*

Fire Trucks and Hats

Focus

Reasoning about algebraic relationships

Summary

Students analyze the elements of repeating patterns and make and test conjectures about hidden elements.

Goals

- Make and test conjunctures
- Reason inductively to generalize patterns
- Reason deductively to identify parts of patterns
- Represent patterns in different ways

Mathematical Connections

Algebra
- Identifying patterns
- Describing and generalizing patterns

Prior Knowledge

- Constructing and extending repeating patterns
- Identifying shape patterns

Analyze how both repeating and growing patterns are generated

Materials

- A copy of the blackline master "Fire Trucks and Hats" for each student, plus one for demonstration
- Two-to-three-inch-square pieces of dark construction paper to represent the doors of a fire station. Make a set of twelve "doors" for each student, plus one set for demonstration.
- A pocket chart or another method of displaying patterns to the whole group
- A pair of scissors for each student

p. 32

Investigation

Engage

Before the lesson, construct a repeating pattern using pictures of fire trucks and firefighters' hats, cut from the blackline master. Place the arrangement on a chalk tray, tape it to a chalkboard, or pin it on a bulletin board.

Call on students to describe the pattern and identify the group of objects that repeats. Do the same for three or four different repeating patterns. You could use one of the following repeating patterns: ABABAB…, AABBAABBAABB…, ABBABBABB

Explore

Tell the students that they will be playing a little game called "Fire Station Doors." Have the children close their eyes while you make a pattern and cover each truck and hat with a "door." When the students open their eyes, have them look at the fire station doors. Explain that they must try to figure out which object—a truck or a hat—is behind each door. Call on students one at a time to choose one of the doors to open, and ask them to describe what they see. (See fig. 1.) After each door has been opened, ask questions like the following:

- (*Point to the next door.*) "What do you think is behind the next door? Why?"
- "Raise your hands if you think a fire truck is behind this door." (*Point to the door.*) "How do you know whether it is a hat or a truck when you can't see it?"
- "Do you agree with the prediction that (*supply student's name*) made? If you do agree, point your thumb up. If you don't, point your thumb down.

"Doing mathematics involves discovery. Conjecture—that is, informed guessing—is a major pathway to discovery."
(NCTM 2000, p. 57)

Fig. **1.**

A repeating pattern of fire trucks and firefighters' hats

Once all the hats and trucks have been revealed, lead students to extend the pattern by asking questions such as the following:

- "What will come next?"
- "What will come after that?"
- "How can you be sure?"

Distribute a copy of "Fire Trucks and Hats," a pair of scissors, and twelve fire station doors to each student. Have the students cut out the pictures of the fire trucks and the hats along the dashed lines and then use the pictures to make patterns. Call on students to describe their patterns. Use students' patterns to play "Fire Station Doors" again.

Once the students are able to identify the elements of the patterns that repeat, talk about other ways in which patterns can be represented. Begin by using the trucks and hats to construct a pattern. Suggest that the students make the same pattern with letters of the alphabet. Ask, "How can you use the letters to show the same pattern?" Encourage the students to use two different letters to identify patterns. Truck-hat-hat-truck-hat-hat, for example, could be shown as ABBABB or CDDCDD or BXXBXX. You may want to create letter patterns and have the students create truck-and-hat patterns to match them.

Extend

Some students may demonstrate an interest in continuing to play the game. The cutout fire trucks, firefighters' hats, and doors (mounted on heavy tagboard or cardboard and laminated for extended use) could be placed in a math center so that students can play the game in pairs.

The applet Making Patterns on the CD-ROM allows students to create "pattern units" from colored squares and examine the larger patterns that emerge when a unit repeats over a grid.

Discussion

After the students have had experience identifying hidden elements in patterns, talk with them about how many doors they need to open in order to identify the repetitive group of elements. Ask them if certain doors are better to try than others are.

Representing patterns in different ways helps students focus on the structures of patterns. This skill is necessary for generalizing and comparing patterns, abilities that are major components of algebraic reasoning.

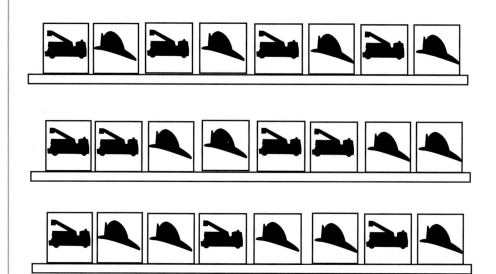

Shape Families

Focus

Reasoning about geometric relationships

Summary

Students describe how the shapes in a group are alike. They identify a shape that does not belong in the group and explain why it does not belong.

Goals

- Reason deductively to identify a common attribute of the shapes in a set
- Describe how shapes differ

Mathematical Connections

Geometry

- Identifying and naming two-dimensional shapes
- Identifying attributes of shapes: straight or curved sides, the number of straight sides, the lengths of the sides (same or different), the type of corners (with right angles or not)

Number

- Counting up to six items

Prior Knowledge

- Recognizing and naming triangles, squares, and nonsquare rectangles in varying positions
- Identifying the straight sides and corners of two-dimensional shapes

Materials

- The twelve shape cards cut from the blackline masters "Shape Cards 1" and "Shape Cards 2," mounted on heavy tagboard or cardboard and laminated for extended use
- A copy of the blackline master "Which One Doesn't Belong?" for each student
- Pencils or crayons for each student

pp. 33, 34, 35

Investigation

Engage

This is a whole-class investigation. Seat the students in a circle. Place the twelve shape cards faceup in the middle of the circle. Name particular shapes, and call on students to find the cards that show the shapes and then give justifications for their selections. For example, ask, "Who can find a triangle?" When a student correctly identifies a triangle, ask, "How do you know that this is a triangle?" (It has three sides.) Direct the student's attention again to the shape cards in the circle, and ask,

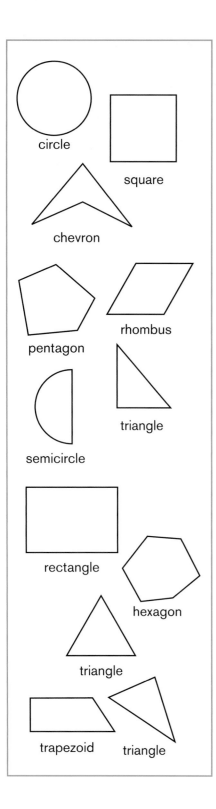

circle

square

chevron

pentagon

rhombus

triangle

semicircle

rectangle

hexagon

triangle

trapezoid

triangle

"Can you find any more triangles?" Next have a student identify the circle and tell how he or she knows it is a circle. Continue by having students point out all the quadrilaterals. Name the square, the rhombus, the rectangle, and the trapezoid, and explain that they are special quadrilaterals. Mention that a square is a special type of rectangle.

Explore

Place all the shape cards faceup in the middle of the circle. Hold up the equilateral triangle, and ask, "Who can find a shape that is like this shape?" After someone correctly identifies a similar shape, probe your students' reasoning by asking a sequence of questions:

- "How are they alike?"
- "Can anyone find another shape that is like this one?"
- "How is this new shape like the first one?"

Follow a similar line of questioning with a shape that is *different* from the equilateral triangle.

The students may attend to different attributes when they select shapes that are alike or different. For example, some students may select the right triangle or the scalene triangle as like the equilateral triangle because the shapes have three sides and are triangles. Other students might say that all the shapes except the circle and the semicircle are like the equilateral triangle because they all have straight sides. The students might also reason that the shapes differ by numbers of sides or that, unlike the equilateral triangle, their sides do not have the same length (i.e., the sides are not congruent).

Place the shape cards for the circle, the square, and the equilateral triangle in the center of the circle. Say, "One of these shapes doesn't belong here," and ask, "Which shape is it?" (circle) Call on a student to identify the shape. Ask, "Why doesn't the circle belong with the others?" If the student says, "It is different," ask for an explanation of how it is different. (The sides are not straight.)

Next, place the square, the rhombus, and the right triangle where they are visible to all the students. Point to the square and the rhombus, and ask, "Why do these shapes belong together?" (Because they both have four sides or four corners.) Ask, "Why doesn't the triangle belong with the others?" If a student responds that it doesn't have four sides (or corners), ask, "How many sides (or corners) does it have?"

For each of the following collections of shapes, ask the students to identify a shape that doesn't belong and give a rationale for their choices. Sample selections and rationales are given. In some cases, your students may offer other appropriate choices and justifications.

- Circle, semicircle, square (The square doesn't belong because none of its sides is curved.)
- Chevron, square, pentagon (The pentagon doesn't belong because it has five sides, and the other shapes have four sides.)
- Chevron, right triangle, and scalene triangle (The chevron doesn't belong because it is not a triangle; it doesn't have three sides.)
- Square, rectangle, trapezoid (The trapezoid doesn't belong because it doesn't have four right-angled corners, so it is not a rectangle. Mention that a square is a special type of rectangle that has four congruent sides.)

Give each student a copy of the blackline master "Which One Doesn't Belong?" and a pencil or a crayon. Instruct the students to draw a ring around the shape in each row that doesn't belong with the others. Do the first problem together, and then have the students complete the worksheet independently. Discuss their answers as a class.

Extend

Students who want a greater challenge may enjoy the following tasks:

1. Put all the shapes into two piles. The shapes in each pile must be alike in some way.

    The students might, for example, place the circle and the semicircle in one pile because their sides are curved and the other shapes in a second pile because their sides are straight.

2. Exclude the circle and the semicircle. Put all the remaining shapes into two piles. Tell how the shapes in each pile are alike.

    For example, the shapes the students put in one pile might have congruent sides and those they put in the other pile might have noncongruent sides, or one pile might have shapes with one or more right-angled (90°) corners and those in the other pile might have no corners with right angles.

Discussion

When you begin this investigation, some students may be able to point to shapes that are alike or different in some attributes, but they may not be able to describe those attributes. For example, some students may perceive that the square and the rhombus are different, but they may not be able to tell you that the difference is that one has right-angled corners and the other doesn't. If the students cannot explain the differences among the shapes, state the relationships for them (e.g., "The square has corners with right angles. The corners of the rhombus do not have right angles"). With experience, the students' descriptions will become more mathematical.

Students who have enjoyed this investigation can continue to explore the properties of polygons with the applet Creating Polygons on the CD-ROM that accompanies this book.

"Being able to explain one's thinking by stating reasons is an important skill for formal reasoning that begins at this level."
(NCTM 2000, p. 123)

Line Up

Focus

Reasoning about measurement relationships

Summary

Students solve logic problems involving the comparison of measurements.

Goals

- Reason deductively
- Make and test mathematical conjectures

Mathematical Connections

Measurement

- Comparing and ordering objects by length and height

Geometry

- Recognizing attributes of shapes
- Using spatial vocabulary

Number

- Using ordinal terms

Prior Knowledge

- Using the following measurement vocabulary to describe comparative lengths and heights: *longer, longest, shorter, shortest, taller, tallest, younger, youngest, older,* and *oldest*
- Using the ordinal numbers and terms *first, second, third,* and *last*

Materials

pp. 36, 37

- A copy of the blackline masters "Line-Up People 1" and "Line-Up People 2" for each student and the teacher. (Each blackline master should be cut on the dotted lines to form the cards.)
- A display board
- A manila folder for each pair of students

Investigation

Engage

Place the three line-up people on a display board, or gather the students in a circle around them on the floor. Name the people as you point to them. Call on students to describe the people. Encourage them to name the people as they describe them. After the students give their general descriptions, ask these questions:

- "Who is wearing plaid pants?" (Drew)
- "Who is wearing a polka-dotted shirt?" (Chris)
- "Who is the youngest?" (Drew)

- "Who is the tallest?" (Chris)
- "Who has the shortest hair?" (Ashanti)
- "Whose hair is longer than Drew's hair?" (Chris's)
- "Who is shorter than Ashanti?" (Drew)
- "Who is older than Chris?" (Ashanti)
- "Who are *not* the tallest?" (Ashanti and Drew)
- "Who are *not* the oldest?" (Chris and Drew)

Explore

Have the students sit in a circle as you demonstrate the first line-up problem. Explain that you will give some clues so that the students can line up the people in the correct order. Tell the students to listen carefully as you read the clues. Then reread the clues, and call on students to help you order the people. Once the figures are in order, read the clues again, one at a time, and have the students check to be sure that the order matches the clues.

Line-Up Problems

1. Drew, Ashanti, and Chris line up to buy tickets for the movies.

   - The tallest person is first in line.
   - The person who is wearing a striped shirt is in the middle.
   - The shortest person is third in line.
     (Chris, Ashanti, Drew)

2. Drew, Ashanti, and Chris line up to buy popcorn.

   - The person with the shortest hair is first in line.
   - The person wearing plaid pants is last.
   - The person with the longest hair is in the middle.
     (Ashanti, Chris, Drew)

3. Next, Drew, Ashanti, and Chris line up to get seats.

   - The person who is not the tallest and not the shortest is in the middle.
   - The person wearing striped pants is last.
   - The shortest person is first.
     (Drew, Ashanti, Chris)

4. After the movie, Drew, Ashanti, and Chris line up to get on the bus to go home.

   - The first person to get on the bus is the youngest.
   - The tallest person is not last.
   - The third person to get on the bus is wearing a striped shirt.
     (Drew, Chris, Ashanti)

Challenge Problems

5. Drew, Ashanti, and Chris line up to get off the bus.

   - The first person is not the youngest.

Drew   Chris   Ashanti

- The oldest person is last.

Who is first? (Chris)

6. Drew, Ashanti, and Chris line up to go in the front door of their home.

- The shortest person is not last.
- The tallest person is first.

Who is last? (Ashanti)

Extend

After a few days of solving these problems as a class, pair the students, and seat them side by side at a table or a desk. Give each pair of students a manila folder and two sets of line-up people. Have the students stand the folder upright on the table or desk so that they cannot see each other's work.

Direct the students to take turns. One of the students arranges his or her three people in a line on the desk, behind the manila folder, and gives directions so that the partner can line up his or her people in the same order. Neither of the partners should be able to view the work of the other until the second lineup has been completed. Then the partners check to see if the order of the second set matches the order of the first.

Some students may have difficulty comparing the orders when they have lined up their figures in different orientations. (One student, for example, may have lined up the people from left to right, whereas the other may have lined them up front to back.) Encourage the partners to point to each person in the lineups as they compare the orders.

If the orders do not match, the partners should try to figure out the reason for the discrepancy. It may be that the clues allow for different correct answers, that no correct answer is possible, or that the students interpreted a clue differently. You may need to assist the students in determining just where the problem lies.

Discussion

Line-up problems challenge young children to reason through multicondition problems and to verify their solutions by checking them against the clues. In line-up problems 1–4, three clues are given, one for each person, but only two are required to solve the problem. The extra clue helps the students focus on each of the people and serves as an additional means of verification.

Problems 5 and 6 present only two clues. The students must deduce the position of one of the people from the information given about the other two. Making inferences about relationships is an important aspect of the problem-solving process and of reasoning, in particular.

Glyph Gallery

Focus

Reasoning about data relationships

Summary

Students interpret and create glyphs—pictorial representations of data.

Goals

- Interpret displays
- Make and justify conjectures

Mathematical Connections

Data Analysis

- Organizing and displaying data

Geometry

- Recognizing attributes of shapes

Prior Knowledge

- Identifying basic shapes
- Drawing basic shapes

Materials

- An overhead-transparency copy of the blackline master "Joe, Anne, and Fred" or an enlarged copy of "Joe, Anne, and Fred" drawn on chart paper
- A copy of the blackline master "A Data Source" for each student
- Paper, pencils, and crayons for each student

Investigation

Engage

Display or project the copy of the blackline master "Joe, Anne, and Fred." Arrange the students in a semicircle to examine the faces at the top of the display. Call on students to name the people and tell how they are alike and how they are different (e.g., both Anne and Fred have four hairs on their heads, but Joe has five hairs; both Joe and Anne have square eyes, but Fred's eyes are triangles). Have the students describe what they see below each face (candles on a cake, pizzas, and houses).

Explain that the pictures below the faces give us clues to what the different features on the faces, or "glyphs," mean.

Explore

Have the students look at the faces and the drawings below the faces. Analyze the glyphs with them by posing the following questions:

- "Which picture—the birthday cake, the pizza, or the house—tells you how old Joe is?" (the birthday cake—it has five candles)

Make and investigate mathematical conjectures

Develop . . . mathematical arguments

pp. 38, 39

- "Which part of Joe's face do you think tells how old he is?" (The hairs on his head—there are five hairs.)

- "How old is Joe?" (five)

- "How did looking at Fred's and Anne's faces help you decide?" (The number of hairs on their heads also matches the number of candles on their cakes.)

- "What part of the faces tells whether the person is a girl or a boy?" (The shape of the face. Anne's face is oval, and the boys' faces are round.)

- "How do you know that a long mouth means that a person likes pizza?" (Joe's is the only face with a long mouth, and there is a pizza below his glyph. The other two have short mouths, and the pizzas below their glyphs have been crossed out. So mouth length and pizza go together.)

- "Look at Fred's and Anne's faces. How do you know that the shape of their eyes tells about the color of their houses?" (Both have four hairs and four candles on their birthday cakes, so both must be four years old. Both have short mouths and both have the picture of the pizza crossed out, so neither likes pizza. Besides the shape of their faces, the only thing different is the shape of their eyes and the color of their houses, so the eyes must tell about the house color. Triangular eyes must represent a white house, and square eyes must represent an orange house.)

Display the glyphs of Kit and Sam. Tell the students that these glyphs follow the same rules that the glyphs of Joe, Anne, and Fred did. Start with the glyph of Kit, and ask questions like the following:

- "Is Kit a boy or a girl?" (a boy) "How do you know?" (His face is round.)

- "How is Kit's picture like Joe's?" (They both have long mouths.)

- "How is Kit's picture different from Joe's picture?" (The pictures differ in number of hairs and the shape of the eyes.)

- "How old is Kit?" (three)

- "Does Kit like pizza?" (yes)

- "What color is Kit's house?" (white)

Ask the same questions about Sam. (Sam is a girl. She is six years old, and she does not like pizza. She lives in an orange house.)

Discuss with the students how they would draw pictures of a six-year-old girl who likes pizza and lives in a white house. (Her glyph would have six hairs, an oval face, a long mouth, and triangular eyes.) Do the same for a seven-year-old girl who likes pizza and lives in an orange house. (Her glyph would have seven hairs, an oval face, a long mouth, and square eyes.)

With the students, create a legend for the features on the glyphs for Joe, Anne, and Fred. Show the symbol for each attribute, and describe what it represents (see fig. 2).

Talk about other facial features that could represent information about people on glyphs—for example:

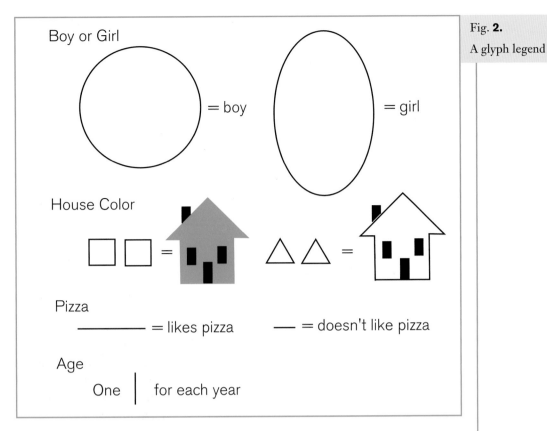

Fig. **2.**

A glyph legend

Boy or Girl

= boy   = girl

House Color

= =

Pizza

———— = likes pizza   — = doesn't like pizza

Age

One | for each year

- Ears, noses, and eyebrows of different shapes
- Eyes of different colors
- Curly or straight hair

Show, for example, what a glyph of Joe might look like if the face color represented the house color, the shape of the nose indicated whether the person is a girl or a boy, the shape of the ears indicated the age, and the shape of the mouth indicated whether the child likes pizza. Figure 3 shows new glyphs of Joe, Anne, and Fred, in which the color of the face matches the house color; a square nose represents a boy, and a round nose represents a girl; round ears indicate a four-year-old, and rectangular ears represent a five-year-old; and a straight mouth indicates a preference for pizza, and a curved mouth means a dislike of pizza.

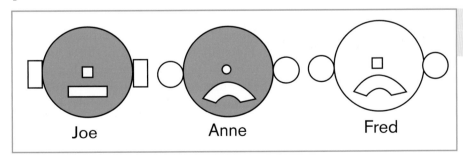

Joe   Anne   Fred

Fig. **3.**

New glyphs of Joe, Anne, and Fred

Extend

As a follow-up, you might either (1) distribute "A Data Source" to each student and ask the students to create glyphs to represent the data shown (see the student-created glyphs in fig. 4) or (2) have the students collect data and create glyphs to represent them. Suggest that the students work in pairs on the extension.

Fig. **4.**
Student-created glyphs

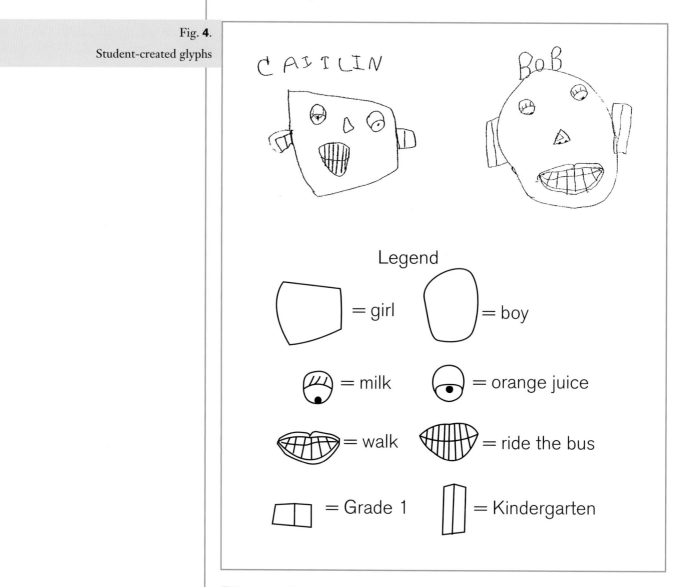

Discussion

Glyphs are an interesting tool for organizing and displaying data. Deciding the number of categories to use and which feature will represent each category demands high-level reasoning. To interpret glyphs, students must compare them and identify similarities and differences. They must compare the "facts" (e.g., the person's name, whether he or she likes pizza or not, the number of candles on the birthday cake, and the color of the house) and deduce how the features on the glyphs are related to the facts.

Navigations Series

Pre-K–Kindergarten

PROBLEM SOLVING *and* REASONING

Looking Back and Looking Ahead

Navigating through Problem Solving and Reasoning in Prekinderarten–Kindergarten shows how young students can be introduced to several problem-solving strategies and reasoning methods. It explores the application of these methods and strategies to the solutions of problems involving number, algebra, geometry, measurement, and data. As students model story problems and decide whether to add or subtract to solve the problems, as in Bears in the House and in the Park, they learn how to reason about number relationships. They reason analogically to identify problems that can be solved in the same way. In an algebraic investigation such as Fire Trucks and Hats, they construct repeating patterns and learn to extend and generalize those patterns. They learn how to inspect and analyze the attributes of two-dimensional objects and how to deduce common characteristics in a geometric investigation like Shape Families. Students make and test mathematical conjectures and reason deductively to solve logic problems involving heights and other attributes of people in an investigation like Line Up, which highlights relationships among measurements. Investigations such as Glyph Gallery, in which students create and interpret glyphs, encourage students to collect and examine data and use them to make and justify conjectures. Throughout the investigations, students learn the importance of verifying solution strategies and solutions.

In grade 1, students will continue to develop their problem-solving strategies and reasoning methods as they apply what they have learned to new settings with more-challenging tasks. They can reason deductively and compare the magnitudes of numbers as they complete stories in which numerical data have been removed and must be restored. In

27

algebraic investigations that involve such activities as making replicas of creatures, they can learn to reason about proportional relationships. From the locations of shapes in the regions of Venn diagrams, they can deduce relationships among two-dimensional shapes. First graders can reason deductively as they use measurement clues to identify locations on a map. Students can learn to interpret and analyze pairs of bar graphs that show the same types of information collected on different occasions, and they can make conjectures about the variability of the data. As in all the grades, students in grade 1 should verify solutions and provide justifications for their choices of solution strategies.

PROBLEM SOLVING *and* REASONING

Pre-K–Kindergarten

Appendix

Blackline Masters and Solutions

The Teddy-Bear House

Name _____

Navigating through Problem Solving and Reasoning in Pre-K–Kindergarten

The Teddy-Bear Park

Name _____

Fire Trucks and Hats

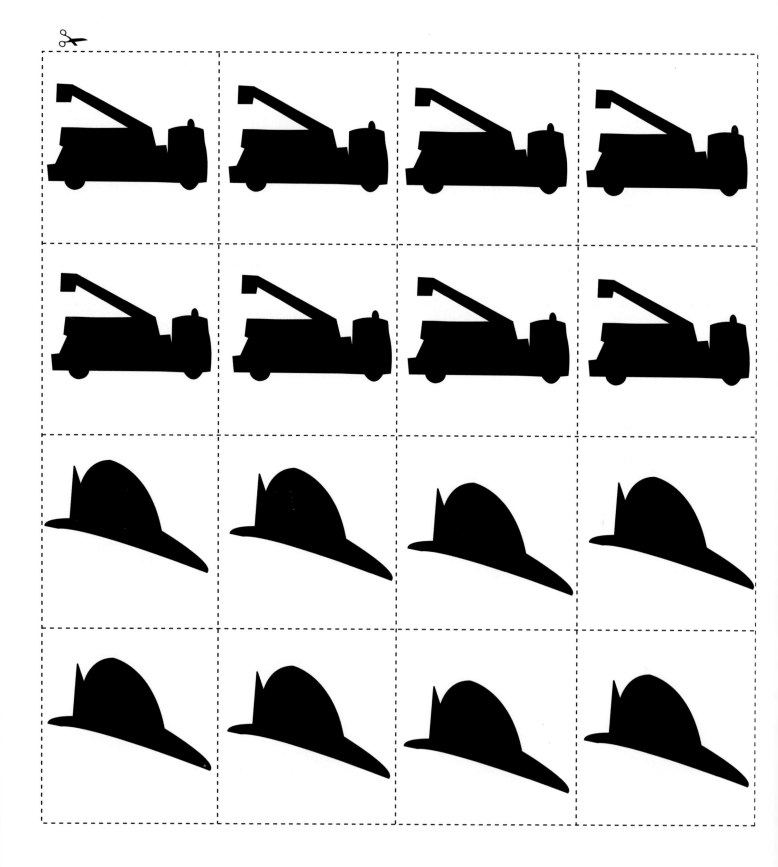

Navigating through Problem Solving and Reasoning in Pre-K–Kindergarten

Shape Cards 1

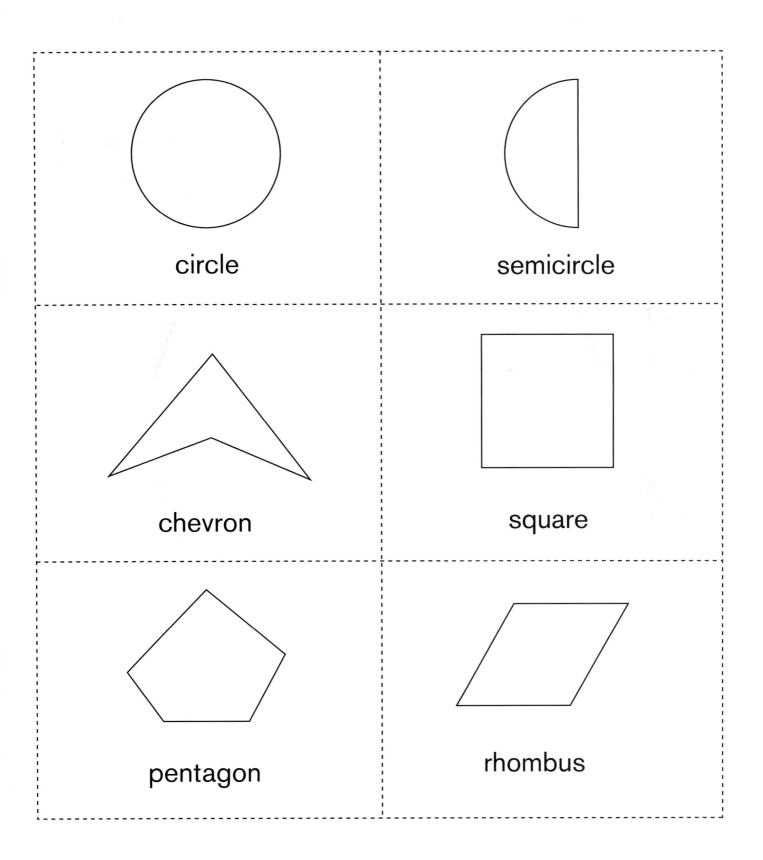

circle

semicircle

chevron

square

pentagon

rhombus

Shape Cards 2

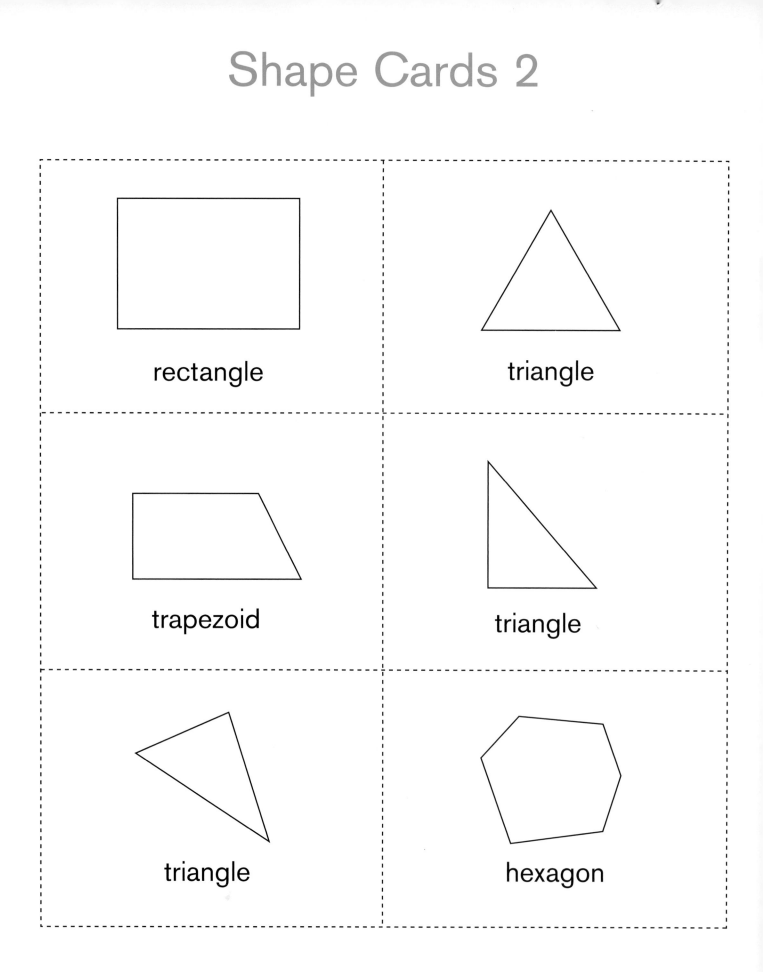

rectangle

triangle

trapezoid

triangle

triangle

hexagon

Navigating through Problem Solving and Reasoning in Pre-K–Kindergarten

Which One Doesn't Belong?

Name _____

Draw a ring around a shape in each group that doesn't belong with the others.
Tell a friend why you think it doesn't belong.

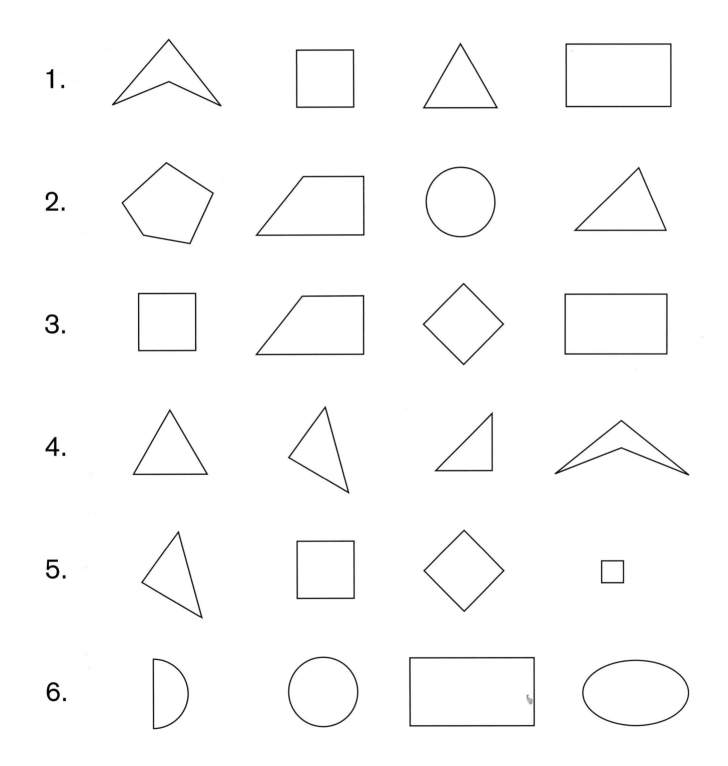

1.

2.

3.

4.

5.

6.

Line-Up People 1

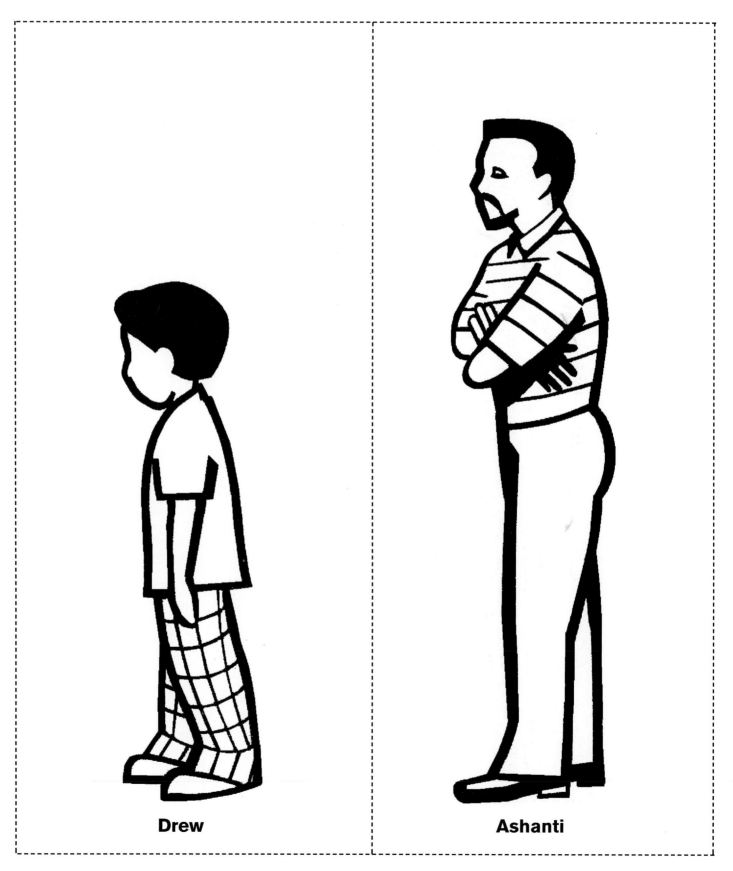

Drew

Ashanti

Navigating through Problem Solving and Reasoning in Pre-K–Kindergarten

Line-Up People 2

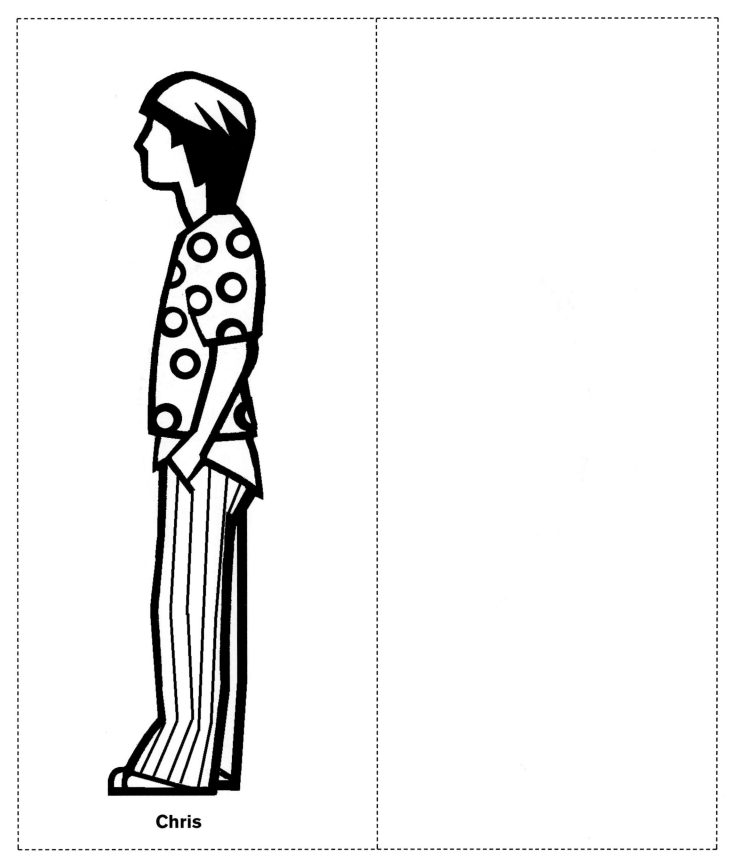

Chris

Joe, Anne, and Fred

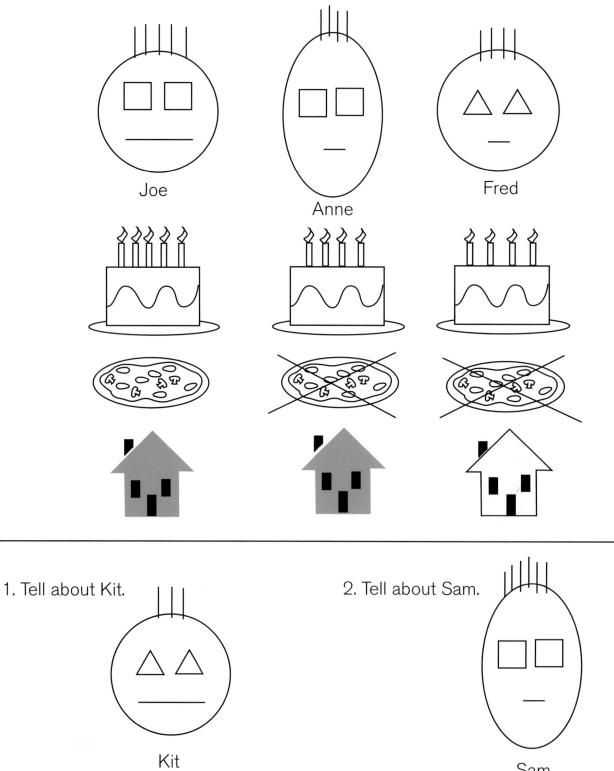

Joe

Anne

Fred

1. Tell about Kit.

Kit

2. Tell about Sam.

Sam

Navigating through Problem Solving and Reasoning in Pre-K–Kindergarten

A Data Source

Names _____

_____

Draw glyphs to represent the data about these students. Draw legends for your glyphs.

1.

	Andy	Mia	Nicki	Tom
Age	3	4	4	6
Brothers	2	3	0	1
Sisters	1	0	1	2
Eye color	Blue	Blue	Green	Brown

2.

	Bob	Caitlin	Jorge	Pat
Favorite food	Pizza	Pizza	Hamburger	Chicken
Favorite drink	Milk	Milk	Juice	Soda
Grade in school	K	K	K	1
Way of getting to school	Bus	Bicycle	Bicycle	Car

Solutions for Blackline Masters

Only the worksheet "Which One Doesn't Belong?" has specific answers.

Solutions for "Which One Doesn't Belong?"

Students' responses and rationales may vary. The following are samples. Listen to students' reasons for their choices to assess the validity of their arguments.

1. The triangle doesn't belong because it has three sides (or three corners), whereas the other shapes have four sides (or four corners).

2. The circle doesn't belong because its side is curved and the other shapes have straight sides.

3. The trapezoid doesn't belong because it is the only shape that is not a rectangle.

4. The chevron doesn't belong because it is the only shape that is not a triangle.

5. The triangle doesn't belong because it is the only shape that is not a square.

6. The rectangle doesn't belong because it is the only shape that does not have at least one curved side.

References

Greenes, Carole, Mary Cavanagh, Linda Dacey, Carol Findell, and Marian Small. *Navigating through Algebra in Prekindergarten–Grade 2. Principles and Standards for School Mathematics* Navigations Series. Reston, Va.: National Council of Teachers of Mathematics, 2001.

National Council of Teachers of Mathematics (NCTM). *Agenda for Action.* Reston, Va.: NCTM, 1980.

———. *Curriculum and Evaluation Standards for School Mathematics.* Reston, Va.: NCTM, 1989.

———. *Principles and Standards for School Mathematics.* Reston, Va.: NCTM, 2000.

Van de Walle, John A. *Elementary and Middle School Mathematics: Teaching Developmentally.* 5th ed. Boston: Allyn & Bacon, 2004.

Suggested Reading

Ameis, Jerry A. "Stories Invite Children to Solve Mathematical Problems." *Teaching Children Mathematics* 8 (January 2002): 260–64.

Atkinson, Sue. *Mathematics with Reason: The Emergent Approach to Primary Maths.* Portsmouth, N.H.: Heinemann, 1992.

Bamberger, Honi, and Patricia Hughes. *Great Glyphs Around the Year.* New York: Scholastic, 2001.

Banchoff, Thomas F. "The Mathematician as a Child and Children as Mathematicians." *Teaching Children Mathematics* 6 (February 2000): 350–56.

Becker, Jerry P., and Shigeru Shimada, eds. *The Open-Ended Approach: A New Proposal for Teaching Mathematics.* Reston, Va.: National Council of Teachers of Mathematics, 1997.

Bird, Elliott. "What's in the Box? A Problem-Solving Lesson and a Discussion about Teaching." *Teaching Children Mathematics* 5 (May 1999): 504–7.

Cobb, Paul, Erna Yackel, Terry Wood, Grayson Wheatley, and Graceann Merkel. "Creating a Problem-Solving Atmosphere." *Arithmetic Teacher* 36 (September 1988): 46–47.

Curcio, Frances R., and Sydney Schwartz. "What Does Algebraic Thinking Look Like and Sound Like with Preprimary Children?" *Teaching Children Mathematics* 3 (February 1997): 296–300.

Dacey, Linda, and Rebeka Eston. *Show and Tell: Representing and Communicating Mathematical Ideas in K–2 Classrooms.* Sausalito, Calif.: Math Solutions, 2002.

Dacey, Linda, Carol Findell, Carole Greenes, and Rika Spungin. *Groundworks: Reasoning about Measurement—Grade 2.* Chicago, Ill.: Creative Publications, 2003.

Dacey, Linda Schulman, and Rebeka Eston. *Growing Mathematical Ideas in Kindergarten.* Sausalito, Calif.: Math Solutions, 1999.

Findell, Carol, Linda Dacey, Carole Greenes, and Rika Spungin. *Groundworks: Reasoning about Measurement—Grade 1.* Chicago, Ill.: Creative Publications, 2003.

Findell, Carol R., Marian Small, Mary Cavanagh, Linda Dacey, Carole E. Greenes, and Linda Jenson Sheffield. *Navigating through Geometry in Prekindergarten–Grade 2. Principles and Standards for School Mathematics* Navigations Series. Reston, Va.: National Council of Teachers of Mathematics, 2001.

Frakes, Cyndi, and Kate Kline. "Teaching Young Mathematicians: The Challenges and Rewards." *Teaching Children Mathematics* 6 (February 2000): 376–81.

Ginsburg, Herbert P., Carole Greenes, and Robert Balfanz. *Big Math for Little Kids: Prekindergarten*. Parsippany, N.J.: Dale Seymour Publications, 2003.

Ginsburg, Herbert P., Noriyuki Inoue, and Kyoung-Hye Seo. "Young Children Doing Mathematics: Observations of Everyday Activities." In *Mathematics in the Early Years*, edited by Juanita V. Copley, pp. 88–99. Reston, Va.: National Council of Teachers of Mathematics; Washington, D.C.: National Association for the Education of Young Children, 1999.

Greenes, Carole. "Ready to Learn: Developing Young Children's Mathematical Powers." In *Mathematics in the Early Years*, edited by Juanita V. Copley, pp. 39–47. Reston, Va.: National Council of Teachers of Mathematics; Washington, D.C.: National Association for the Education of Young Children, 1999.

Greenes, Carole, and Carol Findell. *Groundworks: Algebraic Thinking, Grade 1*. Chicago, Ill.: Creative Publications, 1998.

———. *Groundworks: Algebraic Thinking, Grade 2*. Chicago, Ill.: Creative Publications, 1998.

Kajander, Ann E. "Creating Opportunities for Children to Think Mathematically." *Teaching Children Mathematics* 5 (April 1999): 480–86.

Leitze, Annette Ricks. "Connecting Process Problem Solving to Children's Literature." *Teaching Children Mathematics* 7 (March 1997): 398–406.

Myren, Christina L. "Encouraging Young Children to Solve Problems Independently." *Teaching Children Mathematics* 3 (October 1996): 72–76.

Schielack, Jane F., Dinah Chancellor, and Kimberly M. Childs. "Designing Questions to Encourage Children's Mathematical Thinking." *Teaching Children Mathematics* 6 (February 2000): 398–402.

Sheffield, Linda Jensen. "Creating and Developing Promising Young Mathematicians." *Teaching Children Mathematics* 6 (February 2000): 416–19, 426.

Sheffield, Linda Jensen, Mary Cavanagh, Linda Dacey, Carol R. Findell, Carole E. Greenes, and Marian Small. *Navigating through Data Analysis and Probability in Prekindergarten–Grade 2. Principles and Standards for School Mathematics* Navigations Series. Reston, Va.: National Council of Teachers of Mathematics, 2002.

Sophian, Catherine. "Children's Ways of Knowing: Lessons from Cognitive Development Research." In *Mathematics in the Early Years*, edited by Juanita V. Copley, pp. 11–20. Reston, Va.: National Council of Teachers of Mathematics; Washington, D.C.: National Association for the Education of Young Children, 1999.

Whitenack, Joy, and Erna Yackel. "Making Mathematical Arguments in the Primary Grades: The Importance of Explaining and Justifying Ideas." *Teaching Children Mathematics* 8 (May 2002): 524–27.

Young, Cindy, and Wendy Maulding. "Mathematics and Mother Goose." *Teaching Children Mathematics* 1 (September 1994): 36–38.